The 1 Verse Poetry Collection

ABRIDGED PREVIEW EDITION

Wrong.

AN INSPIRATIONAL POETRY COLLECTION

SAMEER KOCHURE

sameer(@)channelinghigherwisdom(.)com

B19, Sangam CHS, Sai Baba Road,

Off SV Road, Santacruz West,

Mumbai - 54, India.

Author photo by Ahsan Ali.

Written and Published by Sameer Kochure.

Wrong. / Sameer Kochure / First Edition / Paperback

ISBN 978-93-5493-091-1

CONTENTS

PRAISE FOR SAMEER KOCHURE'S BOOKS

"It's a soothing read... it instantly puts a smile on your face! :)"

- Amazon review

"Very cute and same time educating book. I recommend it to everyone... if you had a bad day or a good one."

- Amazon review

"Very nice collection of stories about big questions of life, presented in a very delightful and easy to consume way. I would definitely give it to my teenager kids to read it as well!"

- Peter, Goodreads review

"And all of a sudden, the memory of my loved ones flashed back. The story went straight to my heart."

- Amazon review

“Sameer has distilled the "WISDOM OF THE MASTERS" in just about 100 pages ...It is as if the message is for you as you needed it, at this point of time ...Please do read this book to evolve spiritually. This book will make you happy.”

- Amazon review

“This book takes you back to childhood. It just feels like your mum is telling you stories, teaching you life lessons in the most beautiful and simple manner.”

- Amazon review

“People who follow this (book) are seldom sad and that's something I think more people need to do. We all have this Universe within us, but many people have completely lost touch with it. This book helps you reconnect with it and be content.”

- Ashar Khan, Dubai.

“A light insightful read into every human mind. The book connects to the child in everyone and answers the issues faced by every adult. A must have on every kindle for the days when child like wonder is needed the most."

- Amazon review

"This was a wonderful spiritual story about the friendship between a young boy and the universe. A story about how to think differently than you might at this time and how to appreciate what is around you. It may answer some of your questions, ease your fears or make you look at life differently, no matter what situations arise."

- Alison, Goodreads

To Aai, my mom,

Sunanda Pramod Kochure,

whose love, words and wisdom are

the poetry of my soul.

SOUNDTRACK

Spotify playlist: Ever wondered - *'If this book was a song what would it sound like?'* Wonder no more. Go to https://bit.ly/3WrkjZf or scan the QR code below and enjoy author curated Spotify playlist that perfectly compliments this book. You can even listen to these songs in the background while you read, that's how I wrote it. :)

AUTHOR'S NOTE

Thanks for getting this book, dear reader. I have put together this little edition just for you.

It took precedence over my other projects, because I wanted to say thank you. Thanks for reading my books and supporting me on this journey.

You, the reader, gives meaning to my work as an author. So, I figured, what better way to reward you than with something you love getting - a new book.

So here's a new collection of my free form style of poetry. These poems started life as video content for my social media, but they demanded a book to home them instead.

These poems also don't follow the conventional rules, rhythm, meter or rhyme (although some of them have sneaked up on these pages). Following the convention has never been my forte.

I would rather live a simple, happy, inspired life.

That's what I hope the following pages inspire you to do as well - Live an unconventional life, build your dreams your way, and define your own success and happiness.

That's my wish for you.

I hope you enjoy this book. Play nice even if you don't okay, it's the thought that counts, right?

I love hearing from my readers, so I look forward to your frank, honest feedback. Raving reviews will be tolerated too. :)

And I hope you are on my email list already. If you aren't, you are missing out! Get on my VIP Readers List at www.channelinghigherwisdom.com

That way you'll always be the first to know of my upcoming books. I love pampering my readers with some awesome, behind the scenes bonus content. And I don't want you to miss out on all the fun, so join in, okay?

Alright, off you go now, on to the good stuff.

Love,

Sameer Kochure.

26th May, 2021.

NASA's Voyager 1 has detected plasma waves vibrating in interstellar space.

When converted to a frequency audible to the human ear, a strange rhythmic, humming sound can be heard.

Could it be the Universe speaking to us in poetry?

CHAPTER 1

PRICE TAGS

now i may be wrong
i have been wrong often before
but i believe the time has come
to stop buying expensive things
now i'm all for luxury
and all against a sense of lack
but here's another fact
when we buy a supercar or caviar
30-year-old vintage
or a can of pop...
it doesn't cost us
the money we spend on it
we actually pay for it
with the amount of life
we trade for it.

the barter system
never went out of style
it just came better disguised
imagine how different
the price tags would look then
if they reflected
the true cost of things
would you buy that shiny new car
if the price tag read...
miss 4 birthdays of your kids...
or if it cost you a marriage?
and what if it were
to cost you your ethics?
the price tag looks
quite different now, doesn't it?
i am not here to bash the rich
trust me, it's better to love the rich,
for you can never be anything
that you first don't love
with all your heart,
your subconscious
will make sure of it...
we are just here to understand
the true cost of things
that villa may also come from a book
that's born of your creativity

maybe a song you compose
after your boring 9 to 5
maybe it comes from
a battery you build
in the garage on weekends,
the one that charges itself
while it runs, or
something equally crazy cool
the price tag doesn't look so bad
now, does it?
whatever it costs,
the point is this
the same price tag
may mean different things...
so the next time
you open your wallet
recognise the small pieces of life
you are pulling out of it
and if you aren't spending them
on something truly worthy of them,
then why... oh why,
why are you spending?
the guardians of the economy
the runners of this world
they all want you to always
feel a deep sense of lack

they want you to feel unfulfilled,
not loved enough...
not good enough,
simply
not. enough.
because they know
it is the unhappy souls
who head to the markets
with big carts
and empty hearts
hoping to buy happiness
off the shelf at aisle 17...
and this is why this scam works...
buying happiness - actually works...
...to an extent
...and for a few fleeting moments
that's why your smile widens
when you unwrap
the next newest gadget
or inhale the new car smell
for the first time
but just like that fragrance,
that kind of happiness is short lived
sometimes it lasts a week
sometimes not even a day...
the real happiness in your life

comes from pursuing your
soul
goals
the things that add meaning
to your life
the ones that make
the world a richer place...
so, what are soul goals?
let's turn the page
and find out, shall we?

CHAPTER 2

YOUR SOUL GOALS

now i may be wrong,
i have been wrong often before
but i believe the only way
to be truly happy
is to pursue your soul goals
so what are soul goals?
here are a few examples...
you want to write that book
not because you want to write it
but because
there is something in you
that won't rest till it is expressed...
it wants to... strike that
it demands to be born
you want to build a business

not just to make it to forbes 500
but because you genuinely want
to solve a problem
for the world
you want to teach...
not just to teach,
but to guide and
inspire young minds...
those are the kind of goals
your soul craves
the ones that will bring you
lasting happiness
and notice another
common theme?
these goals,
that make you feel great
just thinking about them,
they had nothing to do with
the amount of money you'll make
because even the pursuit
of these goals makes you richer
it pays you back
not just in money,
although great money
is magically attracted
to the ones devoted

to their soul goals...
it pays you back in something
infinitely more valuable...
it pays your back in
more life energy
it puts a bounce in your step
it twinkles with happiness in your eyes
even if you are not worldly successful
pursuing them just yet...
these soul goals
make you a happier person
because you are living your purpose
even in your pursuit
you are fulfilling them...
these soul goals make you
a better father, a better wife,
a better brother
a better citizen of the world
unlike other things
in the marketplace
that you pay for with
chunks of your life
these soul goals pay you back
with more life in your life
so tell me,
do you want to continue

chasing success the same old way?
and settle for happiness
with a low shelf life?
or are you ready to welcome
the true happiness and abundance
that only comes through living
your soul goals?

CHAPTER 3

HURTS OR HEALS

now i may be wrong,
i have been wrong often before
but i believe
there are only two kinds
as far as relationships go
one that hurts you oh...
and one, that heals you so
doesn't matter the name it carries
or how old or new it seems
a relationship
is a relationship
as long as it involves you
and someone you see... as not you
some relationships
bring wine and smiles

and some,
feel like horrible crimes
some make you walk taller
some make you feel smaller
some you are born into
some you make
some are like morning sunshine
and some...
are like the darkest caves
and while they tell you
to accept them as your fate
i believe to course correct,
it is never too late
this ship that is your life
has one captain
and that's you
you have certainly come
far and wide
and braved
some of the fiercest tides
strong and capable
you still are
and even now,
you are in charge
the real power
is not between

staying and walking...
the real power
is in questioning -
if relationships
are only two kinds,
the ones that hurt
and the ones that heal...
then how can i,
the mighty captain
of my own ship
turn the tides
of something that hurts
into something that heals?

CHAPTER 4
FAME AND FINE

now i may be wrong,
i have been wrong often before
but i believe, being famous
is sometimes better
than being the best
now before you accuse me
of being shallow and being vain
answer me this -
and trust me
i am not going insane
how good is
the best doctor in the world
if no one knows
about him or her?
sure she has the best medicine

and perhaps
he can heal all your wounds
but what if all the patients
that he could save, and so help
never know her name?
does he really exist then?
what if she is easy enough
to be found...
but rarely is he ever found
what if he has a website
and even youtube...
but with only 34 total views?
how useful are her gifts then,
if they stay with him unclaimed?
now, let's talk about
the other one
the one not so gifted,
but a fairly well-known one
now, his cures and her medicines
may only be the second best
his touch may not be as gentle
as the best one
but who among
the two do you think
will end up healing the most?
the best doctor

that cures but a handful
or the second-best healer
that heals the world full
who do you think
will make a greater impact?
now this is not a call
for being famous
over being effective
remember,
the more famous doc above
is still the second best
and here's the thing,
even the second best,
is also known as - one of the finest
so, do me a favour
whatever be your gift
saving lives or
making them more beautiful
forget being the best -
give it a rest
just give
a great energy instead
to being one of the best,
one of the very finest
and what is leftover
of your energy

spend it on promoting
your wonderful self
for that's how
your gift can spread
for your gift is meant to be shared
and that's why
you were given it
when you welcomed it
not to cling, save and hoard,
but to share it sevenfold.

CHAPTER 5

WORDS ON WORDS

now i may be wrong
i have been wrong often before
but i believe the words we speak
don't come out of our mouths
the words we use
come out of our minds
for what are our thoughts
but unspoken words
that only we get to hear
and what are our spoken words
but our thoughts...
that others get to hear
if a person's eyes
are the windows to their soul
then their words

are the mirrors to their minds
our words always say more
than what they mean
they carry
a deeper meaning and convey
the 'not so conscious' feeling
there is no
'oh, i didn't mean anything by that...'
if it is too frequent,
know that it is part of a pattern
there are no innocent words
there are only intentional words
never you be the one
to doubt the power of words
for the concept
of books and libraries
has lived longer
than some of the civilisations
and even some religions
so to really know yourself,
to really understand
the true state
of your inner being
pay a little more attention
to your own words
the ones you say to others

and the ones
you say to your self
notice any common themes?
what do the majority
of them speak of?
do they speak
of hope and cheer?
or do they sound
warning bells of fear?
do they inspire and empower?
or do they drain and
weigh you down?
the real enemies
to your inner bliss
are doubt and fear
and, sadly,
they come armed with
some of the biggest
dictionaries out there
so don't let their
rich vocabulary fool you
they are not as innocent
as they sound
and they are far from fact
when they speak of
doom and gloom

you would be wise
to get a new dictionary
of your own
the one filled
with words of love and hope
there are a gazillion definitions
of happiness out there
and at least a million of them
that will feel just right
as they roll off
your mind's tongue
...
um...
...mind's tongue?
clearly i'm running
out of words there
so i am going to stop right here
here's a heartfelt appeal
before you go though
listen a tad more carefully
to your own words
and correct them
while they are just words
'cos the life
you've created for yourself
and the world you see out there

it's made up of your thoughts
and your words
because your words
are the bricks
that build your life...
and your world.

CHAPTER 6

QUESTION THE QUESTIONS

now i may be wrong
i've been wrong often before
but i believe the only way
to get a really good answer
is to ask a really good question
of course you know this,
but indulge me a bit,
i'll even say, pretty please?
people see the simplicity
and the beauty of a great solution
but they often forget
to acknowledge
the most important step
to reaching it
- starting with

a really good question
here's an example of two ways
of defining the same problem
why can't i afford it?
how can i afford it?
see the difference
between the two?
it's not the words
that are different
it's the thought process
one reflects
a scarcity mindset
the other comes
from a resourceful mind
let's work on
another problem together -
why can't i enjoy
loving relationships
in my life?
now, let's reframe
the question to -
where am i not loving myself?
better than
the original, right...
let's see if we can
make it even better

how about -
what is within me that is
stopping me from loving me?
good, good,
we are getting there....
how about this -
how can i love myself
so much that
i only attract good things to me?
ah, i like that last one,
don't you?
it's the same problem,
just understood better
better questions = better answers,
that's how it always works
better questions
force your mind
to look at the problem sideways
and from different angles
you'll find hidden in those
different perspectives
the right solution
to the issue
that caused
the original problem
the problem is rarely

what it appears to be
often the seeds
to today's problems
are sown in
yesterday's experiences
treat the cause and
the effects heal
by themselves
makes sense, right?
strike that,
let me ask you
a better question -
which areas of your life
will get better,
if you start
asking better questions?
oh, i like that last one...
let me leave you to
ponder on it a bit.

CHAPTER 7

THOUGHTS ON THOUGHTS

now i may be wrong
i have been wrong often before
but i believe
the crimes of the worst kind
are often committed
in our own mind
everything i have lived
read and studied
right from
the long lost ancient texts
that were magically rediscovered
to the teachings of the buddha,
the bhagvad gita
and even napoleon hill
all the timeless knowledge

and the wisdom in the world
tells me the biggest error
a human being can make
is to think in an incorrect way...
so, what is the correct way?
the truth is,
our mighty mind,
as vast and as limitless as it is
it is big enough
to hold only one
single dominant thought
at a time
so which dominant thought
do you hold the most?
the one of faith
or the one of fear?
the thought that a good life
is possible even for you, my dear
that you actually deserve it
that you are good enough,
worthy enough
or is that dominant thought
shivering in the dark
and whispering of lack?
is it telling you, you are unworthy,
undeserving, unqualified

not so pretty, not so rich,
not so ________
you know how to fill in that blank.
this, my friends,
is the incorrect way of thinking
now i'm not asking you
to put on rose-tinted glasses,
and say that
the blue sky is pink
neither am i asking you to
bury your head in the sand
and pretend your problems
do not exist
i know they do, they are true
and as real as are you
but here's another
truth about you
you are bigger than anything
you could ever face
you are the centre of your universe
you are the flame in every fire
you are the light of the sun
you are the love of the moon
you are the most powerful being
in your own world
there's no problem

that you could ever face
that you won't be able to
overcome with grace
so start with a little faith
in your own divine self
stand strong, stand your ground
stand for you, stand with you
own your own life
own your power
and above all
own your own mind
after all, that's your
most precious real estate
don't let any weeds of lack
fear and doubt
grow in your mind
plant seeds of faith
self love and self belief
water them daily,
care for them
and watch them grow
and it won't be long
for those seeds to take root
and for your life
to bloom
for there is nothing

in this universe
that can't be yours
if you will just take the time
and put in the effort
to set your mind right first.

CHAPTER 8

THE FAILURE TRACK

now i may be wrong
i've been wrong often before
but i believe
one of the best things
you can do in your life
is to make best friends
with failure
now failure is often misunderstood
looked down upon
and people do their best
to avoid crossing it
in life's corridors
but the truth is,
trying to avoid failure
is the shortest path to failure

they say
man often meets his destiny
on the path he takes to avoid it
i believe
the same can be said about
trying to avoid failure
the fact is you only
fail at something
if you fail to learn
the lesson from it
for every failure
carries with it a gift
that can't reach you without it
and it is these gifts
that will eventually
chart your way to success...
failure is not a label not a person...
it is a school, it is life's tuition
so here's my take
take all you can from failure
fail more, fail often
fail louder, fail harder
fail all you can,
and then fail some more
when you think you can't
because the more you fail,

the more you'll pave the way
the more you fail
the more the risks you'll take
the more you fail
the more the dreams
real you'll make
here's another fact
we didn't come wrapped
in bubble-wrap
we were not made
just to play safe
otherwise we would never grow
out of our mother's embrace
for where else
did we really, really feel safe?
success has a great appetite
and a good taste
it feeds on failure
and hungers for more of it
failure is its vitamin,
failure is its nutrition...
so don't put
success on a diet
make failure your best friend
and it won't be very long
before success

wants to join you two,
and your happy gang
for that's when
success comes calling
not when you
go after it chasing
but when you get
real comfortable failing
so stop running after success
and away from failure...
start running after failure
and watch in wonder as
success comes running after you.

CHAPTER 9
FAULT FINDERS

now i may be wrong
i've been wrong often before
but i believe, one of the best things
we can do for others
is to be the best version
of our own self first
it's easy to find faults and see
how things could be better
...in others.
and it's just as difficult
to be honest and true
about the mistakes
and shortcomings of you
the self - the one true one,

is whole and complete as is
it's the form,
the physical bits of you
that need a little work
and yes, for the purpose
of this exercise
count your emotions,
and your ego,
to be physical too
often they are
just as out of control,
and as fallible, as are you...
when you focus on you
and see the mountain
of task before you
you'll go easy on asking others
to change so readily too
and as you go to work
on being your better self
the ones surrounding you will
auto-magically change
for the better too
...or get replaced
by their better versions
that's how these things work
a lotus growing in the mud

makes a pond
where there was only mud
so will your environment change
to be in tune with the new you
all these wonderful things happen
when you are busy
building a better you
books, workshops,
journaling, exercise,
healthier habits and food...
you are smart,
you already know the way
this is one of those rare times
when being selfish
is actually good
...and if that
makes you hesitate,
since you are so good at
taking care
of others - over you,
then do it
for them instead.
that's how we started,
as you will remember...
now i may be wrong
i've been wrong often before

but i believe,
one of the best things
you can do for others
is to be the best version of
your own self first.

CHAPTER 10

THE BEAUTY OF YOU

now i may be wrong
i've been wrong often before
but i believe,
it is not your face
but your flaws
that make you beautiful
diamonds are precious
not for how fine they look
but because you know that
the light dancing in them
came from a stone
that was rough cut
by our own mother earth
the ads, the 'gram and the tube
they will all tell you

to hide that nose
even to have no nose
if you can
to puff up those lashes and
pinch your cheeks
before you take that pic
but rarely will someone tell you
how beautiful you really look
when you cheer someone up
who was feeling down
or pick someone up
who slipped
and fell on the street
now that's a thing
of real beauty, and rarer too
still, you'll find it in every city,
on every single day
and in every home...
even your own.
more likely than not,
you'll find that beauty
staring at you
in the mirror too...
...with eyes hungry
for some of your love
so forget your compact

or cologne... and put on
some compassion instead
it may not win you
beauty pageants
or make you social famous
but trust me,
it will win you the right hearts,
...the ones that truly matter.

*

Dear Reader, thanks for reading this short and sweet poetry collection. I hope you enjoyed it.

While I believe these poems carry an important message, I deliberately kept this collection short.

I believe, the best poems have a strong emotional core. Poems that live in the real world and are rooted in truth.

That's why, I want take a minute to talk about my other two books in this series that I feel you will enjoy as well.

The first one, **'Made of Flowers and Steel'** is about women, and the second one **'Tough Skins, Tender Hearts'** is about men.

Made of Flowers and Steel

Inspired by true stories, this book is a poetic celebration of the raw grit and tenacity that it takes to be a woman in today's world.

It's never been easy to be a woman. Unimaginable challenges stand in their way. Yet, time and again, no matter the odds, they rise to the challenge and put up a fight worthy of honour.

And they conquer.

I believe it is time to celebrate that fire. The steel beneath the beauty.

Welcome to a poetry collection that celebrates the strength behind the beauty that is a woman.

Inspired by stories of real women, **this collection of 100 poems honours the raw grit and the moral fortitude that exists in all women.** Sometimes that power is inherent, sometimes it needs to be invoked, but it is always there.

Page after page, you'll discover a newfound love and respect for yourself, and for all the women in your life.

Written by Sameer Kochure, the author of the much adored book series *'A Young Boy and His Best Friend, The Universe,'* and *'Wrong. - An inspirational poetry collection,'* this book is an uncompromising, powerful work of art.

It's NOT a regular book of poems on love, heart-break or feminism. **It's a salute to the moral strength it takes to be a woman** in today's world. The steel beneath the flowers.

An empowering and a comfort read for all the thinking, feeling women around the world. And for everyone who loves them.

Turn the page to read a few poems.

CHAPTER 12
AMBUSH

when anxiety
ambushes you
and gives you a chill...
look it in the eye,
give it your sweet smile
and say,

'you can't get me silly...
don't you know,
i am made of flowers and steel?'

CHAPTER 13
THE BLUE BOWL

i still hear those words, dad
just the way you said them...
i even remember the way you looked
that beautiful summer day...
funny how memories work, right?
i don't remember what
i had for breakfast this morning
but i hear those words from 21 years ago
just as i heard them for the first time
as i stood at the sink
looking at the broken bowl
that had slipped through
my tiny soapy fingers...
you didn't even sound angry
as you said,

'you really can't
do anything, can you?'
i remember the rainbow lights
dancing in the foam becoming brighter
by the tears in my eyes.
i am sure you forgot all about
that bowl before the day,
or the week was out
while i came to know
that blue bowl intimately
as it stayed with me for 2 decades...
long it used to cut and stab me
especially when it was time for me
to do something new...
first job, first kiss, first labour...
that bowl, and those words
would come and find me, right on cue
filling me with doubt
'how can i do this
if i can't do anything?'
it took a whole lot of self love,
caring and nurturing by kind
and loving souls to win me back
my lost confidence
in time, i learnt to bury
that blue bowl and let go of it

but the words remain.
they still mock me
whenever they feel like...
hoping to catch me by surprise.
but now, i have
a fitting answer for them.
whenever they ask
'you really can't do anything, can you?'
i just smile and say, 'watch me.'

i look like i am made of flowers,
but i am really made of steel.

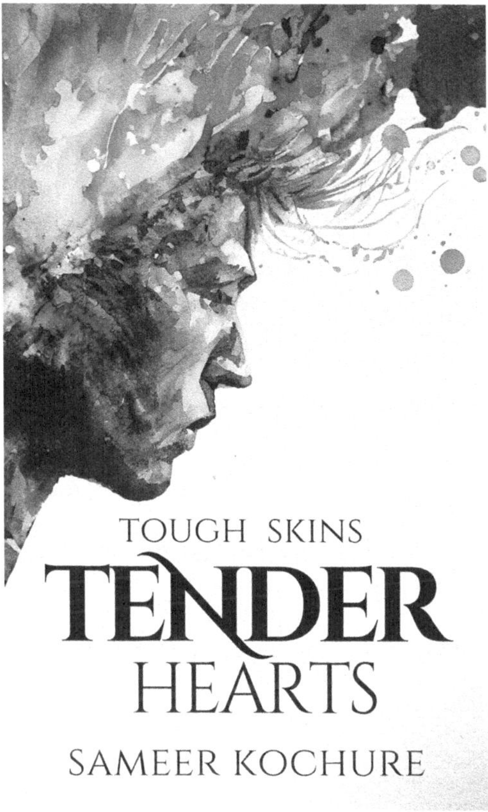

The mind tells us beautiful stories,

But a man's heart lays bare the truth.

— SAMEER KOCHURE

Welcome to an unveiling, an understanding, an unravelling of the man's heart.

As painlessly as possible, we will rip open a

man's ribcage and put the soft, quietly beating muscle under our microscope, in an effort to unlock its mysteries.

What will we find?

Perhaps some hope, some desires, some fears.

A few battle hardened scars, way too personal dreams, wounds yet to heal, maybe a tender moment or two.

Maybe something more?

Let's go and explore.

Buy Tough Skins, Tender Hearts

Turn the page to read a few poems.

CHAPTER 15
TETHERED

not gonna lie
your cute smile, pretty face
and sparkling eyes,
that's what
caught my attention
at the first glance
but the eyes that light up
when they meet mine
the heart that makes mine blush
and the soul that sings,
dances and vibes with mine,
now that,
that's what
keeps me tethered to you.

Get Tough Skins, Tender Hearts

CHAPTER 16
ABSOLUTE CHAOS

i wonder what are you doing
at this very moment...
the moment i am thinking of you.
right here, right now.
pray tell me, what are you up to?
besides, of course,
turning things upside down,
throwing everything sideways
burning all maps,
jamming all gears, derailing all plans,
causing utter chaos and dysfunction...
please oh please, do tell,
what are you doing right now besides
starting a protest, a movement, a
rebellion

in the deepest recesses of my heart?

Read all 96 poems.

Get your copy of Tough Skins, Tender Hearts

SOUNDTRACK

Spotify playlist: Ever wondered - *'If this book was a song what would it sound like?'* Wonder no more. Go to https://bit.ly/3WrkjZf or scan the QR code below and enjoy author curated Spotify playlist that perfectly compliments this book. You can even listen to these songs in the background while you read, that's how I wrote it. :)

ALSO BY SAMEER KOCHURE

Get amazing bundle deals on official author website:

www.ChannelingHigherWisdom.com

The Tiny Fireball

A cute, wholesome, comfort-read sci-fi fantasy featuring star-crossed lovers.

A Young Boy And His Best Friend, The Universe — Volumes 1–10.

Comfort-read short stories that answer life's toughest questions—including the ones keeping you up at night.

Made of Flowers and Steel

An empowering poetry collection that celebrates the raw grit and inner strength of women.

Tough Skins, Tender Hearts

Poems about men, for everyone who loves them.

LOVED THE BOOK?

Hated it? Found it 'meh'? Adored it?

Tell the world.

Leave a short review on your favourite sites that'll help readers like you. A good deed… and all that :)

ABOUT THE AUTHOR

Author photo by Ahsan Ali

Sameer Kochure was born in India during the darkest part of the night. Probably explains why he is such a self-proclaimed dreamer. He has lived in 6 cities and 3 countries since. He has also clocked in 15+ years as a Creative Director in some of the biggest advertising agencies across Asia Pacific. He lives in Dubai, but claims that anywhere he travels, he feels he is home.

You can know more and join his VIP mailing list at:

www.ChannelingHigherWisdom.com

BUY OR BORROW

Libraries played a big part in nurturing my love for reading while growing up. So to give back some of the love libraries have shown me, I have made sure that all my books are easily accessible to major libraries across the world. In case, you can't find my books at your library, just fill out a simple book request form, all libraries have them, and more often than not, they will be happy to procure them for you and honour your request. They love supporting loyal readers like you. Libraries are awesome that way. Show them some love as well. :)

ACKNOWLEDGMENTS

All my books could not have been written without the love and support of my family, Dr. Monica, Dr. Narahari, Hriday, Viju Maushi, Tayade Uncle, Gau, Pinks, Sam, Ishaan; and my spiritual guides and teachers, you know who you are. Know also that I am nothing; and with your guidance and blessings, I do everything. To all of you, I give thanks. To you my reader, you complete the circle, I give thanks. And finally, to my homie, the Universe, I give thanks.

GRATITUDE

Thank you for reading.

You are a true friend of the Universe.

Printed at Repro India Ltd.